THRASS®
TEACHING HANDWRITING READING AND SPELLING SKILLS

THRASS® 500 SERIES
DICTIONARY

Alan Davies & Denyse Ritchie

Illustrated by Terry Allen

THRASS DICTIONARY

The THRASS DICTIONARY is a workbook.
Words from reading and spelling activities
are stored in this workbook for reference.

THRASS®

Revised Edition 2002
First published in 1998 by
THRASS (AUSTRALIA) PTY LTD & THRASS (UK) LIMITED

UK
Units 1-3 Tarvin Sands
Barrow Lane
Tarvin
Chester CH3 8JF
England

Tel. 01829 741413
Int. +44 1829 741413
Fax. 01829 741419

© Alan Davies & Denyse Ritchie 1998
ISBN 1 904912 12 5
Product Code T-12

www.thrass.co.uk

THRASS®
DICTIONARY

CONTENTS

HOW TO USE THIS DICTIONARY

FINDING WORDS

Listen to the one-minute Vowel Phoneme Sequence on the THRASS RAPS AND SEQUENCES CD and 'tap' under the 20 vowel phoneme-boxes on the THRASS PICTURECHART (ISBN 1 904912 02 8) until you are familiar with the 20 vowel phonemes.

Listen to the two-and-a-half-minute Grapheme-Word Rap (Vowels) and 'tap' under the 60 vowel THRASSWORDS until you are familiar with the words and their vowel graphemes. These graphs (one-letter-spelling choices), digraphs (two-letter-spelling-choices) and trigraphs (three-letter-spelling-choices) are highlighted in bold print on the chart.

Look at the words listed on the 'ant' page, (page 6). Say all of the words aloud. The first vowel phoneme in each of these words is that heard at the start of the word 'ant'.

Now look at the words listed on the 'baby' page. Say all of the words aloud. The first vowel phoneme in each of these words is that heard in the word 'baby'.

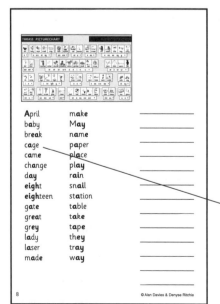

The words 'ant' and 'baby' both contain a vowel graph 'a' but they represent different vowel phonemes. Therefore, the words 'ant' and 'baby' will be found in different word lists in this dictionary. The word 'rabbit' has two vowel phonemes (therefore two syllables) but the first vowel phoneme is the same as that heard at the start of the word 'ant'. Hence, the word 'rabbit' is found on the 'ant' page.

The word 'cage' has the same vowel phoneme as that heard in 'baby' and is, therefore, found on the 'baby' page. The words 'day' and 'snail' contain different vowel digraphs but they will also be found on the 'baby' page.

The words 'break' and 'eight' both contain the vowel phoneme heard in the first syllable of 'baby'. However, the digraph 'ea' in 'break' and the quadgraph 'eigh' in 'eight' although not illustrated on the charts are represented by an asterisk, called a Grapheme Catch-All or GCA. These graphemes appear in the GCA Box.

Apart from the words listed as Non-Phonographic Spellings (pp 46-47), the first vowel grapheme in each word is in bold print.

ADDING WORDS

SAY THE WORD and listen for the first vowel phoneme.
SAY THE FIRST VOWEL PHONEME.
DECIDE on the graph, digraph, trigraph or quadgraph that represents the phoneme.
FIND the page for the phoneme.
WRITE the word on the page and name the letters.
OVERWRITE (trace over) the first vowel grapheme and name the letters.

GRAPHEME CATCH-ALL

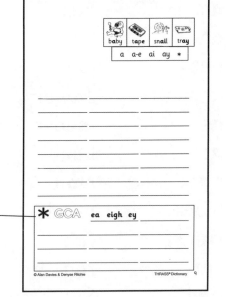

The THRASS PICTURECHART (or GRAPHEMECHART (ISBN 1 904912 03 6) does not include every vowel grapheme. There are hundreds of graphemes that represent the 20 English vowel phonemes, therefore the THRASS charts would be difficult to use if they were all included. Graphemes not included on the chart are represented by an asterisk, called the Grapheme Catch-All or GCA. If the word you are adding to a list contains a vowel GCA, write the new spelling choice in the GCA Box.

If desirable, vowel GCAs (and, if you wish, consonant GCAs) can be added to a separate GCA SHEET, located in the READING SECTION of the THRASS RESOURCE FILE (ISBN 1 904912 01 X).

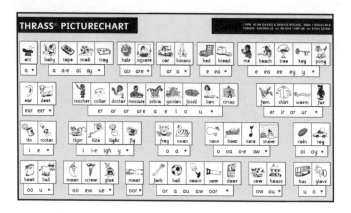

am	happy
an	has
and	have
ant	jam
animals	January
as	ladder
at	lamb
back	man
black	panda
can	rabbit
cat	ran
dad	Saturday
had	tap
hammer	than
hand	that

ant

a   *

---

* GCA

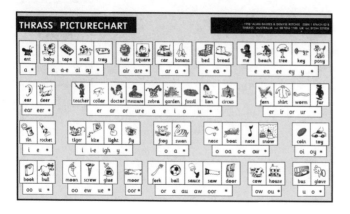

April	m**a**ke	_____
b**a**by	**M**ay	_____
br**ea**k	n**a**me	_____
c**a**ge	p**a**per	_____
c**a**me	pl**a**ce	_____
ch**a**nge	pl**ay**	_____
d**ay**	r**ai**n	_____
eight	sn**ai**l	_____
eighteen	st**a**tion	_____
g**a**te	t**a**ble	_____
gr**ea**t	t**a**ke	_____
gr**ey**	t**a**pe	_____
l**a**dy	th**ey**	_____
l**a**ser	tr**ay**	_____
m**a**de	w**ay**	_____
		_____
		_____

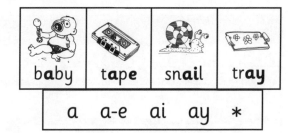

baby	tape	snail	tray
a	a-e	ai	ay	*

_____ _____ _____

_____ _____ _____

_____ _____ _____

_____ _____ _____

_____ _____ _____

_____ _____ _____

_____ _____ _____

✱ GCA ea eigh ey _____

_____ _____ _____

_____ _____ _____

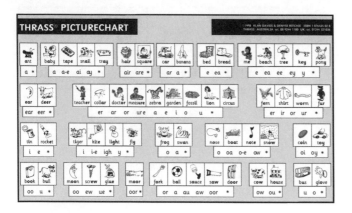

bear

chair

fair

hair

pair

pear

square

their

there

where

_____

_____

_____

_____

_____

_____

_____

_____

_____

_____

h**air**	squ**are**

air are ＊

_____ _____ _____

_____ _____ _____

_____ _____ _____

_____ _____ _____

_____ _____ _____

_____ _____ _____

_____ _____ _____

＊ GCA   **eir ere ear** _____

_____ _____ _____

_____ _____ _____

_____ _____ _____

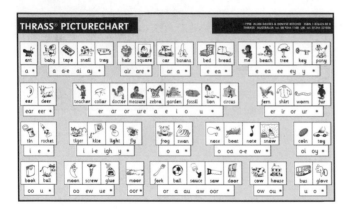

after

are

asked

can't

car

father

garden

half

heart

last

laugh

March

park

shark

started

car | banana

ar a *

_____ _____ _____

_____ _____ _____

_____ _____ _____

_____ _____ _____

_____ _____ _____

_____ _____ _____

_____ _____ _____

* GCA   are ear au al

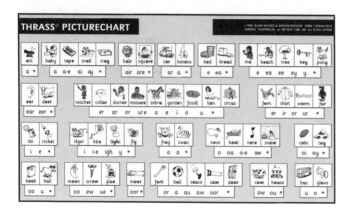

any	h**e**dge	s**e**ven
b**e**d	h**e**lp	s**e**venteen
b**e**ll	l**e**g	t**e**n
b**e**tter	l**e**ft	th**e**m
br**ea**d	l**e**tter	th**e**n
ch**e**rry	m**a**ny	tr**ea**sure
ch**e**f	m**ea**sure	tw**e**lve
dr**e**ss	m**e**t	tw**e**nty
egg	n**e**t	v**e**ry
end	n**e**ver	W**e**dnesday
every	n**e**xt	w**e**nt
f**ea**ther	r**ea**dy	wh**e**n
F**e**bruary	r**e**d	y**e**llow
f**e**lt	s**ai**d	y**e**s
fr**ie**nds	s**ay**s	z**e**bra
g**e**t	s**e**cond	
h**ea**d	S**e**ptember	

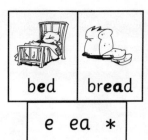

bed | bread

e ea *

---

* GCA   a ie ai ay

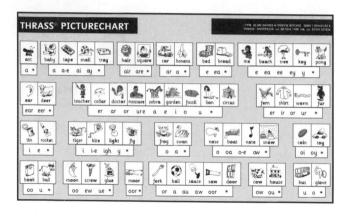

be	meet	teeth	_____
beach	people	these	_____
bee	piece	three	_____
been	please	tree	_____
being	queen	we	_____
cheese	read	wheel	_____
December	sea		_____
eat	secret		_____
field	see		_____
free	seen		_____
green	she		_____
he	sleep		_____
keep	sleeve		_____
key	sneeze		_____
knee	street		_____
leave	tea		_____
me	teacher		_____

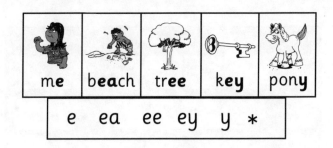

me	beach	tree	key	pony
e	ea	ee	ey	y *

_____ _____ _____

_____ _____ _____

_____ _____ _____

_____ _____ _____

_____ _____ _____

_____ _____ _____

✱ GCA   ie eo

_____ _____

_____ _____ _____

_____ _____ _____

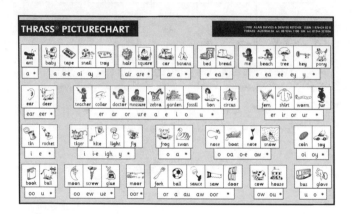

d**ear**

d**eer**

ear

h**ear**

h**ere**

n**ear**

r**ea**lly

w**e're**

y**ear**

z**e**ro

_____

_____

_____

_____

_____

_____

_____

_____

_____

_____

_____

_____

_____

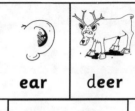

ear | deer

ear eer *

_____ _____ _____

_____ _____ _____

_____ _____ _____

_____ _____ _____

_____ _____ _____

_____ _____ _____

_____ _____ _____

* GCA   ere ea e're e

_____ _____ _____

_____ _____ _____

_____ _____ _____

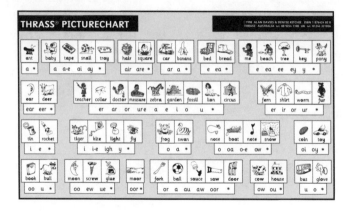

a

about

above

across

again

along

another

around

away

b**a**lloon

b**a**nana

c**o**mputer

h**e**llo

J**u**ly

m**a**chine

o'clock

p**o**lice

th**e**

t**o**day

t**o**gether

upon

_____

_____

_____

_____

_____

_____

_____

_____

_____

_____

teacher	collar	doctor	measure	zebra	garden	fossil	lion	circus

er   ar   or   ure   a   e   i   o   u   *

＊ GCA

THRASS® Dictionary   21

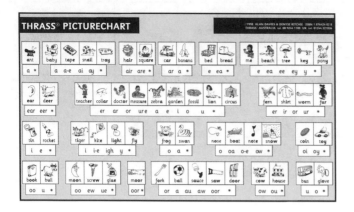

THRASS® PICTURECHART

bird
birthday
circus
earth
fern
first
fur
girl
heard
her
purple
shirt
thirteen
Thursday
turned

were
word
world
work
worm

_____

_____

_____

_____

_____

_____

_____

_____

_____

_____

_____

_____

_____

_____

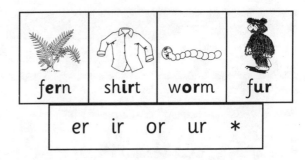

fern	shirt	worm	fur

er	ir	or	ur	*

_____ _____ _____

_____ _____ _____

_____ _____ _____

_____ _____ _____

_____ _____ _____

_____ _____ _____

_____ _____ _____

✱ GCA   **ear   ere** _____ _____

_____ _____ _____

_____ _____ _____

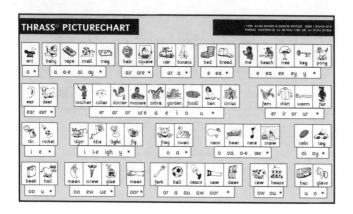

because	fish	quick	———————
before	fizz	quilt	———————
began	give	sister	———————
below	him	six	———————
between	hippo	sixteen	———————
big	his	still	———————
bridge	if	swimming	———————
children	important	think	———————
city	in	this	———————
did	ink	tin	———————
didn't	inside	will	———————
different	is	window	———————
dig	it	with	———————
dinner	king	without	———————
eleven	kitten	wrist	———————
fifteen	little	zip	———————
finger	lived		———————

© Alan Davies & Denyse Ritchie

tin | rocket

i   e   *

_____ _____ _____

_____ _____ _____

_____ _____ _____

_____ _____ _____

_____ _____ _____

_____ _____ _____

_____ _____ _____

* GCA

_____ _____

_____ _____ _____

_____ _____ _____

_____ _____ _____

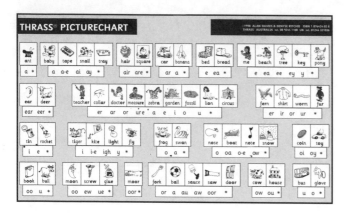

buy	like
by	lion
dinosaur	might
eyes	my
five	night
fly	nine
Friday	nineteen
giant	right
high	tiger
I	time
I'll	tries
I'm	while
ice	white
kite	why
light	write

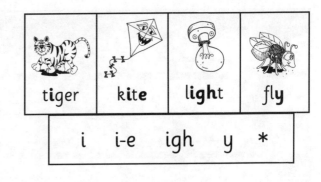

tiger	kite	light	fly

i	i-e	igh	y	*

---

* GCA uy eye ie

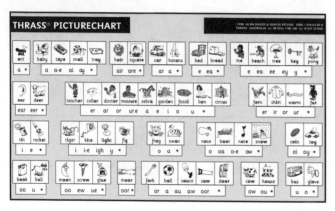

box	**O**ctober
c**o**ffee	**o**f
c**o**llar	**o**ff
c**ou**gh	**o**ften
d**o**ctor	**o**n
d**o**g	**o**range
d**o**lphin	r**o**cket
f**o**llowing	sh**o**p
f**o**rest	st**o**pped
f**o**ssil	sw**a**n
fr**o**g	w**a**s
fr**o**m	w**a**nt
g**o**ne	w**a**sp
g**o**t	w**a**tch
l**o**ng	wh**a**t
l**o**ts	
n**o**t	

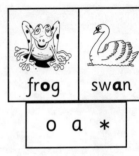

frog	swan

o   a   *

_____ _____ _____

_____ _____ _____

_____ _____ _____

_____ _____ _____

_____ _____ _____

_____ _____ _____

_____ _____ _____

* GCA   ou_____ _____

_____ _____ _____

_____ _____ _____

_____ _____ _____

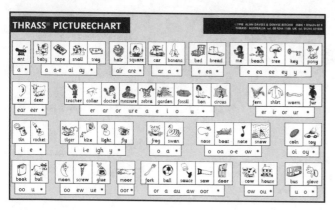

b**oa**t	**o**ld	
b**o**th	**o**nly	
cl**o**sed	**o**pened	
cl**o**thes	**o**ver	
d**o**n't	**ow**n	
g**o**	p**o**ny	
g**oe**s	r**oa**d	
g**o**ing	sh**ow**	
h**o**me	sn**ow**	
kn**ow**	s**o**	
m**o**tor	s**oa**p	
n**o**	th**o**se	
n**o**se	t**o**ld	
n**o**te	wh**ole**	
N**o**vember	w**o**ken	

© Alan Davies & Denyse Ritchie

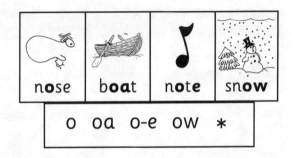

n**o**se	b**oa**t	n**o**te	sn**ow**

o oa o-e ow ✱

---

* GCA   oe

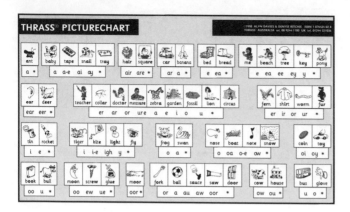

boil

buoy

boy

coin

join

noise

point

soil

toy

voice

_____

_____

_____

_____

_____

_____

_____

_____

_____

_____

_____

coin   toy

oi   oy   *

---

* GCA   uoy

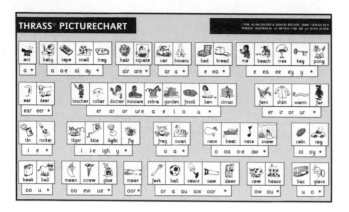

THRASS® PICTURECHART

book

bull

could

foot

full

good

look

pull

push

put

should

took

woman

wood

would

_____

_____

_____

_____

_____

_____

_____

_____

_____

_____

_____

_____

_____

_____

b**oo**k	b**u**ll

oo	u	*

✳ GCA   oul   o

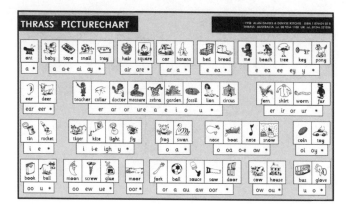

blue

do

flu

fruit

glue

June

moon

school

screw

through

to

too

two

who

you

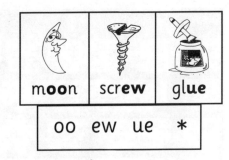

m**oo**n	scr**ew**	gl**ue**

oo	ew	ue	*

✱ GCA   o   u   ui   ough   ou

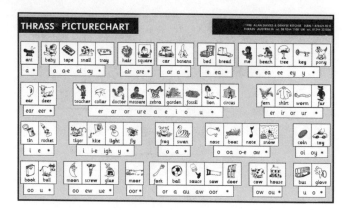

THRASS PICTURECHART

1998 ALAN DAVIES & DENYSE RITCHIE ISBN 1 876424 02 8
THRASS AUSTRALIA tel. 08 9264 1100 UK tel. 01244 331086

m**oor**

p**oor**

p**our**

s**ure**

t**our**

m**oor**

oor *

✳ GCA   **ure**   **our**

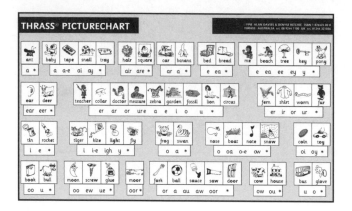

all	**or**	
almost	s**au**ce	
also	s**aw**	
always	sm**a**ll	
August	th**ough**t	
b**a**ll	w**al**ked	
br**ough**t	w**a**ter	
c**a**lled	y**aw**n	
d**oo**r	y**our**	
f**or**		
f**or**k		
f**our**		
f**our**teen		
h**or**se		
m**ore**		
m**or**ning		

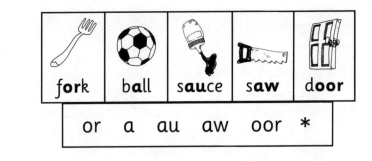

fork	ball	sauce	saw	door

or	a	au	aw	oor	*

_____ _____ _____

_____ _____ _____

_____ _____ _____

_____ _____ _____

_____ _____ _____

_____ _____ _____

_____ _____ _____

* GCA   **ough   our   ore   al**

_____ _____ _____

_____ _____ _____

_____ _____ _____

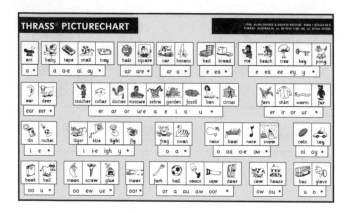

br**ow**n

c**ow**

d**ow**n

f**ou**nd

h**ou**se

h**ow**

m**ou**se

n**ow**

out

outside

owl

pl**ough**

r**ou**nd

sh**ou**t

s**ou**nd

_____

_____

_____

_____

_____

_____

_____

_____

_____

_____

_____

_____

_____

_____

_____

cow | house

ow ou *

---

* GCA   **ough**

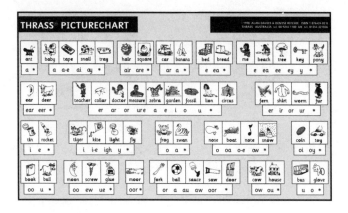

THRASS PICTURECHART

1998 ALAN DAVIES & DENYSE RITCHIE ISBN 1 876424 02 8
THRASS AUSTRALIA tel. 08 9244 1100 UK tel. 01244 221036.

br**o**ther	n**u**mber
b**u**s	**o**ther
b**u**t	s**o**me
c**o**me	s**o**mething
c**o**ming	s**o**metimes
d**oe**s	s**u**ch
d**u**ck	s**u**ddenly
gl**o**ve	s**u**n
j**u**mped	S**u**nday
j**u**st	th**u**mb
l**o**ve	**u**nder
M**o**nday	**u**ntil
m**o**ney	**u**p
m**o**ther	**u**s
m**u**ch	w**o**n
m**u**m	y**ou**ng
m**u**st	

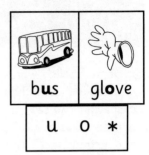

bus | glove

u   o   *

＊ GCA   oe ou

Non-Phonographic Spellings

In some English words the first vowel phoneme is not represented by a grapheme, that is, there is no one-to-one relationship between a sound and a spelling choice. For example, in some words a letter may represent two or more phonemes (e.g. the 'u' in em-u and the 'o' in o-ne and o-nce). The letters 'e''w' in n-e-w and d-e-w are also considered to be NPS words because they are not digraphs but unusual graphs, that is, the 'e' represents the consonant phoneme heard at the start of 'yawn' and the 'w' represents the vowel phoneme heard at the end of 'glue'.

For consonants, the 'x' as in box, often represents the two phonemes heard at the start of k-itten and s-un (i.e. it represents a consonant blend).

Write Non-Phonographic Spelling words on these pages. Say the word and overwrite the letter-string that is the **NPS** and name the letters.

NPS words

Dr	m**u**sic	_____
d**u**ring	n**ew**	
f**ire**	**o**nce	_____
h**our**	**o**ne	
kn**ew**	**our**	_____
Mr	T**ue**sday	
Mrs	**u**sed	_____
Ms		
		_____

NPS? Not Playing Sensibly!

(see T50, TEACHING THRASS, page 71)

_____   _____   _____

_____   _____   _____

_____   _____   _____

_____   _____   _____

_____   _____   _____

_____   _____   _____

_____   _____   _____

_____   _____   _____

_____   _____   _____

_____   _____   _____

_____   _____   _____

_____   _____   _____

Consonant GCAs

Use this page to record Consonant GCAs e.g. <u>b</u>haji, pla<u>que</u>, na<u>t</u>ure

b bb * <u>b</u>haji	
c k ck ch q * pla<u>que</u>	
ch tch * na<u>t</u>ure	
d dd *	
f ff ph *	
g gg *	
h *	
j g ge dge *	
l ll *	
m mm mb *	
n nn kn *	
ng n *	
p pp *	
r rr wr *	
s ss se c ce *	
s *	
sh ti ch *	
t tt *	
th *	
th *	
v ve *	
w wh u *	
y *	
z zz ze s se *	